Finding Self:

Journey to Self-Love

Moonsoulchild

Welcome, to the experience of my **journey to self-love**. I will take you down a very **personal**, **intimate**, and **difficult** path. I found myself lost for many years, trying to discover who I was meant to be. I found myself trying to fit in, trying to stand out. I found myself **confused** most of the time. What I'm going to share with you, is my open heart, praying it will bring a touch of peace to you. I can't speak on anything I haven't once felt, lived, or am currently going through. So, when you're reading, and you take it all in, or find yourself not relating to it, just think of me, a human, with a heart, baring it into each page, trying to bring as much knowledge as I can, to help your road to discovery not seem so lonely. I'm not here to provide the answers for you, I'm here to give you all of me, and my story and hope it either misses you, or you find inspiration in it. I know my story won't fit everyone or anyone, but it has inspired me, and I think if it reaches a least one soul, that's enough for me. So please, don't hold what I say as right, or wrong, it's neither. It's a **raw**, up close, and **personal experience** in my heart, mind, and soul. Get ready, for a **wild** ride. I promise you, if it's one thing you will do, you'll feel it for me, and that alone, will **inspire** you.

Self-love is only **hard** when you put everyone's worth before your own.

Have you ever lessened, or lost your worth being occupied trying to help someone you love, find theirs? It's easy

when you love someone, it's not hard to fall blindly in love, especially if your partner has demons their currently struggling with, it becomes your call to save them (a least that's what you believe is the right thing). You love them, and of course, you would do anything to help them not feel pain, even if the pain was never brought by you, you make it your duty to make their demons disappear.

But let me tell you,

1. *You can't save anyone!*

I've been front and center, I know exactly what it's like to lose myself trying to save someone I love, just to prove my love runs deep, and unfortunately, to make them love me as much as I love them. It landed me in many failed relationships.

- *I put them before my needs*
- *I fought to prove myself*
- *I blamed myself for the pain*

The energy I gave to every argument, or to make them see the heart I have, to see a partnership in me. I spent more time trying to prove my heart than being loved the way I set out to be. I lost interest in everything I once enjoyed, being accustomed to their interests. I lost all sight of my direction because it was my chance at being loved. I blamed myself for the pain when the stories ended. I placed too many good intentions onto someone who wasn't ready for my love because they weren't even ready for themselves. This just made my journey to the self, a whole distance farther. I blamed myself, but only when I was still too blind to see the light. I only blamed myself for trying to prove myself in a situation that only proved no matter how badly I wanted to be loved, I couldn't find my worth fighting someone else's demons, I had to fight my own.

Lessons learned:

- Work on myself first

- Don't try saving **anyone**

- I can't make someone's pain disappear

- My love doesn't need to be proved

- Find my worth before I try finding purpose elsewhere

You know why it's important to not try proving your worth to anyone?
To anyone?
They will always choose what they see of you.

I haven't been in many relationships, but I've had relations with many. Some I casually talked to, and some I forced more. I've been in three real relationships in my lifetime, everything else was just myself trying to prove my love and how much I could give. I thought proving would equal love. I thought having a big heart meant someone would want to share that, I mean, it's rare. It's something out of this world to capture a big heart and to be loved by one. I went far trying to prove this. It didn't matter the relation. You could have been a friend. If you were someone I loved and wanted to hold close, I did everything I could to make that happen.

1. Don't **SETTLE**!

*I say this because once you settle, you become defined by them. You lose yourself by becoming accustomed to their desires and needs, you forget your own. I know when you hear "settle down," you think it's what you do when you find the right one, but that's not how I see it (now at least). I like to say, **grow**. I made a vow to myself to no longer "settle" for anything or anyone! If I can't grow within the relationship, I can't keep them in my life any longer. I refuse to give my energy to anyone who doesn't see the importance of growing. I can't be with anyone or be a friend to anyone who settles.*

2. Don't stress about being "**accepted**"

There was a moment in my life when I cared too much about what someone thought about me. I ended up placing this insecurity among all my relations. What they thought about me made a huge impact on what I thought of myself. I tried to stand out, and I tried to fit in, but neither worked for me. **I realized I was meant to grow at my own pace, and at my own risk.** *It's a lot to separate yourself from the opinions of others, especially the ones you love. They find it easy to belittle you because you love them too, so it's easy to one-up you. This is exactly why I knew trying to prove myself wasn't going to win me, love, in any aspect.*

Here's an example,

I had a best friend, we were inseparable for about 6 years, then we crashed and burned. The love for her is still alive, but it's a thing of the past. We were so close from high school until we reached our 20s. Our lives were taking different directions. I was falling in love for the first time, my first real relationship, as she, was already experienced. She was becoming a mother, a beautiful experience. I stayed with her through her highs and lows. I was always there for her when she needed me. I couldn't always be physically present. I worked two jobs while going to school. Life wasn't how it once was for us. We started to clash more every day. It became a battle. I didn't know how to handle the situation back then, I just tried to hold her close, so I took the fall. I was shamed for living the life I thought I wanted at the time while trying to figure it all out. She lived the life she wanted but couldn't accept me for the same reason. She found every reason to belittle me or prove I was against her. No matter how many times I stayed, went back, or proved my loyalty, it was always overlooked.

Lessons learned:

- *Grow, don't settle*

- *Don't want to be accepted*

- *Proving doesn't get you what you want*

- *Proving doesn't get you ANYTHING!*

- *People are temporary, even after years.*

Don't be afraid to be free,
To be freely who you are.

If you haven't found who that may be,
Don't be discouraged to stop your journey because you're
not clear on where you're at, or where you're going.

I like to think of myself as a free spirit, someone who has an open mind and takes in all perspectives. I like to believe I'm free. I didn't always believe this. I once clouded my mind with the opinions of others. I once found myself at many dead ends. I didn't know what it was like to be "free" because I couldn't define myself unless I was being defined by others. I went through many phases of what I wanted to be, and who I thought I was, just based on their opinions.

One thing,

1. *Don't **give** up!*

Your journey isn't going to happen overnight. It will take years of hard work and dedication. You will be interrupted by many souls who try to change your direction. You will be confused because you find something else to interest you. THIS IS THE PROCESS. ***You aren't born and ready to be this amazing soul. You build your character and become the person you were meant to be.***

Let me break it down for you,

2. *You will fail many times!*

Don't lose hope because you came to a roadblock or many. You will get knocked down many times, but it's important to not lose focus. When you want something, you don't let the "what could go wrong"

stop you, because let's be honest, something can
always go wrong. Something will always go wrong,
but just to test your strength.

3. **Insecurities**, *what are those?*

Battling your deepest insecurities is what holds you
back the most. It's the fear in the back of your mind
telling you that you won't make it. Are you going to
let fear become you? I know, it's easier said than
done. But let me give you an example,

I have battled loving myself for years, I didn't fully
accept myself until I was 25 years old. I battled with
being shy my whole life. I made it a point to stay
quiet most of the time because someone would
always play on the fact I didn't speak. I know you're
wondering, why didn't I stand up for myself. Well let
me explain,

I was quiet for so long that I became a joke.
Everyone thought I didn't have a voice, so how
would I just stand up for myself if I was scared to
speak? I didn't even know where to start, I held my
share of friends who I spoke with, they always held
me down and spoke for me. I was bullied for not
speaking, which also riddled the anxiety brewing
inside me. I was scared to face many bullies without
realizing they have insecurities too. Someone always
had something to say about me, which is funny now,
because I never spoke to give them anything, so
everything was based on their idea of me. Even

though I played it off as if I didn't care it took a lot from me. I started being insecure with other parts of myself. I weighed about 100 pounds until I was about 20, growing up that was also a struggle. I would get body shamed a lot. The winning question is, DO YOU EVEN EAT? People swore they were funny, but deep down inside me, I didn't know what I did wrong to become a platform for everyone's insecurities. Lastly, the insecurity I still struggle with is my skin. I had acne growing up, a lot. it made me feel less attractive, so I tried making it up with my body. I knew I had a decent body, so why not use that instead? Oh, I was wrong. This one situation comes to mind

I liked this boy, this was post-high school, but not long after. We talked a lot before meeting up. Social media was a thing, that's where we met, but he only lived 15 minutes from me. He was a bit older, but at that time, I was just looking for fun. We decided to meet up one day, my friend, him, and his friend all met at the beach. It was a fun time, nothing out of the ordinary. Once he dropped me off at home, about an hour later I received a text from his friend, stating he didn't wish to talk to me again because my skin "**wasn't clear**" yes, this is real, I'm not lying. I tried justifying it. I tried to understand why I wasn't beautiful enough. I also went down the route of him being a piece of shit, but I learned more about not being beautiful. I was placed into many situations to test my worth, to see if I would open my eyes, but I failed. I battled myself for years because I saw the beauty others tried to make me see. I always wished I could see myself in someone's eyes, until that one situation. It made it harder to open myself up to anyone, but also gave me the light, not everyone will think I'm beautiful, all that matters is if I believe I am.

Lessons learned,

- No one can love me as I love myself.

- I may fall, but I will always rise.

- Never let anyone silence me

Everyone struggles with self-love because when self-doubt takes over it seems more powerful.

Self-doubt is your brain throwing curve balls, trying to disturb your peace.

Rise above the doubts,
The demons trying to make loving yourself seem powerless.

Loving yourself is magic.

Self-love is difficult when you're battling yourself. Self-doubt, the fear of the unknown. The fear of not being as great as you believe. Self-doubt takes over when you start comparing yourself to everyone, and anything. Have you ever had that one friend who always had it together? Have you admired a celeb or an influencer?

One thing,

1. *Don't compare!*

The more you compare yourself to someone else or their life, the more you'll fall deeper into doubt. Social media is a place you can meet so many people, you can share your art or your business. Social media is also a place a lot of people can be who they want without the need for approval. If you're someone who gets influenced easily by your surroundings, you should unfollow anyone who makes you feel like you're losing yourself. Don't give your energy to those you compare yourself to on a daily. Ask yourself these questions,

- *Why do I follow?*
- *What am I inspired by?*
- *What are they doing for me?*

These questions are essential. If you're someone who is currently looking for your passion, it's going to be hard to follow accounts that "have it together" I've been there, and I would ask myself, "what do they have that I don't?" without realizing it wasn't my time, nor are we the same. There are many influencers on social media for many different things. Follow those who help your journey, not take away from it.

If you find yourself constantly upset over things these people post or find yourself judging them, unfollow them.

2. It's not them, it's you!

I don't want you to get confused, I'm not blaming you. I'm saying when you're lost it's hard to understand others' success. It's hard to see clearly through jealousy, or self-doubt.

Here's my story,

I have had a passion for writing since high school. I found my inspiration through music, mainly Ne-Yo. I adore his music, along with his songwriting ability. I wanted to write music. I found myself always writing poetry about different emotions I've felt throughout my life. I never shared many of my pieces with anyone. I kept all my work to myself. It was a dream to write a book, but that was at a standstill because I didn't believe I could make that my long-life career at the time or have the means to write one. I was still gaining knowledge.

I wanted to be a therapist.
I wanted to be a marine biologist.
I wanted to be a teacher.
I wanted to work in early childhood.
I wanted to work in the medical field.
I wanted to be a dancer.
I wanted to be a model.

I "wanted" to be many things, but none of those were my dreams. The crazy part, all those things I wanted to be were short-lived because I couldn't find the inspiration or the ability to not doubt myself. I found a problem in everything I did. I couldn't focus. I was lost and I couldn't find the passion. I couldn't understand why I couldn't be great at all the things I wanted. I compared myself to everyone who could. I also compared myself to the "prettier" woman, one I wish I could look like. I let my insecurities play a big part in everything I did because I never had the confidence. I didn't make it known that I had these doubts, so they ate me alive. I went through many different roads trying to find what I wanted and who I wanted to be. I grew into the soul I was meant to, be with the help of my mistakes and failures. I grew confident in myself once I accepted writing as my passion, wholeheartedly. While I was searching for my passion, I also got stuck in finding love. I got lost in someone, so I lost sight of my writing. Once writing and I united, it's been nothing but bliss.

So yes,
I still have doubts, sometimes more about my
appearance than anything else. When it comes to my
writing, not so much. I'm a sensitive soul, so when
someone tries to analyze my work and say it's wrong
or right, knowing I write from experience, it's hard. I
learned not to feed into the ones yet educated on
parts of life I've lived through. I tell my experience
and do not alter it. I should not be insecure about my
work, but the scariest part is putting it out there in
the world and having others label it how they wish,
knowing it can make or break me. I like to believe
I've battled those demons.

Lessons learned:

- *Never compare*

- *Be different!*

- *Find your passion*

- *Eliminate the negative*

Age is just a number,
When it comes to self-love.
There's always more to discover,
Somedays seem like a battle,
Somedays you feel you've concurred the world.

Just know,
You will forever soul search,
The goal is to love yourself even when you're battling
yourself.

Age is just a number when it comes to finding more about yourself or trying to discover self-love. You aren't born loving yourself. The sad part of all, is you grow up loving others more than you can love yourself. This isn't a bad thing, but how can you truly love someone completely without loving yourself first? A question I have always asked myself for years until it finally made sense. You give to everyone you love almost 100% of your time, attention, and heart. You're one call or drive away when someone you love is in need, it becomes first nature. So, you grow all these years trying to make someone love you the same as you give, but it won't work.

1. *You can't force what's in the cards!*

What the universe has planned for you can't be altered, and if it is, it will be flawed. You can't make someone love you. You can't make someone feel on the same level as you do. The more you force what's not meant to be, the more the universe will place you in that situation until you learn from it.

2. *Focus on yourself for once*

Breakups are hard when you invested so many years and so much of your heart with them. So, instead of trying to rewrite history and trying to make sense of why it went wrong, focus on becoming a better you. I can speak this into existence and still have someone say "but I love them" of course you do, love doesn't

disappear. Love will stick with you forever,
sometimes it fades, and sometimes it stays. Love
doesn't mean you hold on. When the story ends, a
new chapter begins, and that chapter is you.

3.   *Soul Search*

Go out.
Meet new people.
Enjoy time in your solitude.
Make a new recipe.
Write in a journal.
Read a book.

You can never do enough soul-searching. It's always
exciting finding something new about yourself.
There's always a battle you face, whether it's with
yourself or a loved one, it will affect you. Each battle
is a new part of you opening a new road of new
beginnings. A test of growth, of strength.

I'm currently 26, it took me 25 years to love
myself, and even now I still struggle with time. I put
myself through many battles I didn't think I would
overcome, but here I am, stronger than ever. I gave
all of what I could to everyone throughout my life. I
always had a genuine, full heart. I also made
mistakes and completely lost signal of who or what I
wanted to be. I have discovered a different part of
life I never knew existed. I have found a place of

peace within myself not many can relate to yet, but I pray they soon claim. I have been heartbroken, let go, and ghosted. I have lived almost every part of the pain you can imagine, yet here I am. I'm proud of who I am and that's a lot to say. 2 years ago, I couldn't even look at myself in the mirror without makeup because I couldn't see the beauty in being natural. I was with someone who couldn't accept me for the sensitive spirit I withhold, so I changed for their needs, so I could be loved. I'm living proof it doesn't take overnight to love yourself. It also doesn't ever end, there's always more to love. I spend more time in my solitude. I spend more time with my loved ones. I surround myself with positive vibes and open minds. One of the biggest lessons I learned, was to accept myself whole, I must see myself through everyone's eyes. I must see all perspectives of who I am to everyone, to know who I am not. I knew I couldn't wake up and be great, I had to own it. I had to create it. I didn't love myself until I let go of those who didn't love me completely. I couldn't love myself while having people who only loved me in half. I am a human of habit, so when I get comfortable or feel safe it's hard to adjust. I hated change. Once I stepped outside of my comfort zone, everything I was afraid of became beneath me. I became fearlessly in love with myself.

Lessons learned:

- *Don't rush to have it all figured out.*

- *Spend time alone*

- *Break out of your comfort zone*

- *Trust the universe*

List *4 things you love* about yourself:

1.

2.

3.

4.

Why?

List 4 things you need to work on:

1.

2.

3.

4.

Why?

You **glow different** when you're happy,
So today,
Find that glow.
Find your happiness,
Let go of what's holding you back.

Self-love *is,*
Every loss loving anyone who made it hard.
It's getting hurt time after time,
Because you thought your love was enough to heal
anyone you tried to make understand your worth.

it's getting broken down just to show you,
The most important person is yourself.

You may feel like you're in a situation currently that won't pass, but a year ago you were also in a situation that felt like no return.

You'll always find yourself in a situation,
Sunk deeper every time.
You'll always survive the storm,
You'll always make it through.

It's never the end. There's always going to be a situation that arises, mainly to test your strength, you need to keep going.

1. *Don't give up!*

It's important to hold yourself together at the times you feel yourself falling most. It's important to watch closely as you get deeper into situations, so you don't lose sight of what you're getting from it.

Many things could interfere with your thought process, one thing mainly is your fears. If you fear the unknown, you'll always fight yourself when it comes to change. Change is inevitable, if you don't like change, it will happen regardless of what you want it to. Change is only scary when you trick your brain into believing whatever is coming next isn't going to be something you can handle.

2. *Don't get comfortable!*

Accept change with open arms. If change scares you, refer to it as growth, because that's exactly what it is. You can't expect to be in the same situation forever if it's not meant to be long-term. You can fight to stay in a relationship that doesn't fit anymore, but you will always end up hurt and confused as to why it's not working. Not every relationship or friendship can't be changed, you can always fight, but if the situation or the person outgrows you, there's no going back. It's important to not stay comfortable, to always know there's more for you.

3.   Stay strong!

When you find yourself in a rut and you ask yourself, why am I still here? I promise you, it's because of your strength. We weren't put on this earth to be weak. We weren't born to be broken. Staying strong through every storm is hard, yes, but it's not so hard when you realize that for every bad thing that comes your way, a bigger blessing comes. Until you defeat whatever it is that comes to test you, the universe will continue placing those same battles until you've learned. Open your eyes.

My story,

I have been through so many hardships, some more simple than others, some not so much. A lot of them I had complete control over, I just chose to not be smart about my decisions. I look past the truth many times. I forgot my strength and let myself become weak in many situations. These situations have helped me grow into the woman I am today, and above all, gave me the experience I needed to correct my behavior and my mistakes.

I lost my grandparents, I was a sophomore in high school (I didn't feel the loss) because I was going through my (If I don't feel it, it will pass) phase.

When I think about them today, all I do is cry. I didn't handle their death properly I didn't give myself the time to heal. Instead, I chose to hide my pain.

Getting my first car repossessed, I was completely depressed. It brought me to the real world. It was a wake-up call to my spending abilities. With the help of loved ones, I got my car back, I also paid back everything I owed to them for helping me. I was young at the time, growing up not having so much education on how to spend money wisely, and it caught up to me. Now, I fully manage my bills and pay them on time or early. I was in a dark place when I didn't have my car, I thought I failed myself. I didn't like that I had to depend on so many others. Sometimes it takes going through something terrible to see the light.

Josie, I lost my dear friend two days before I graduated college. I remember doing my interview in class and going back to my phone to find out the news. I broke down completely, I couldn't drive home for hours. I spent the night with my favorite teacher, she just let me be alone with my thoughts. I couldn't process this alone, of course, so I tried to find anyone close to me to help me. It sucked, no one truly knew her that was close to me, I know that didn't make a difference, but it just didn't feel right to me. It made it so much harder. I was depressed. I had many panic attacks. I tried badly to understand why this was happening, I even blamed myself. I found my way, with the help of her soul and spirit, and her signs. She guided me to the light. I gave myself permission to feel everything. I did everything opposite to when I lost my grandparents. I learned from that mistake. Feeling everything up close was one of the hardest things to do, especially alone, but it was the best thing for me. My heart was broken, but it also mended itself. Feeling is healing. It may take some time, but I pulled myself together.

I could list so many hard times I had throughout my life, but to be honest, how many of us haven't lived through many? We've all been heartbroken. We've all felt like we've lost it all.

A reminder,

*Every day you wake up is a blessing, even if you currently don't feel **alive**. You were meant to overcome every bad day, week, or year. You were given a big heart, not to break you, but to shape you. Pain comes and goes, but some stick with you forever. That's the crazy part about life, it's a mess, but it's also the biggest blessing.*

Lesson learned,

- *Don't stop giving your all*
- *Be Thankful*
- *Forget a comfort zone*
- *Pray*
- *Feel to heal*

Finding Self: *Journey to Self-Love*

*My **Self-love** journey,*

I was always someone who loved more, and who always wanted to show my heart. Not because I wanted to be the one chosen, but more so, because I was someone worth all the love I gave. I never seemed to condition my love. I always gave but never pushed to receive.

I condition myself to believe if I showed my heart and loved wholeheartedly, the love will be reciprocated. I found myself time and time again, in the circle of being the only one loving, or not being loved enough.

I searched. I chased. I tried hard to prove my love to people who only wanted me to love them, but never cared to express their feelings. Some just wanted me close, so that when they were ready to settle down, I might get chosen.

My love wasn't a game, I wasn't going to let someone who couldn't love me back play with my heart and try to make me believe I wasn't worth more. I realized I was important when I realized my heart was too big to love people who didn't care to love me back.

I went through a lot of disappointing times. I put myself in situations I couldn't blame anyone else for the outcome. My heart lived its own life, sometimes it was hard to ignore the love that was beating. I loved people who were wrong for me, and some who never loved me.

I didn't wake up one day and "love myself", I'm going, to be honest, it's hard. It's difficult to love yourself in a world filled with people trying to bring you down. Continuing to prove how many times I put myself out there just to get damaged.

2017 was a year that took a toll on my heart. I lost a close friend. It tore my heart apart. I learned how to cope with grief and move on from someone I had no choice but to only love in spirit. It was a year of learning how to love people from afar. I let go of a best friend I cherished for many years. I became rocky with someone I was with for many years. It was only the beginning of my journey. It opened my eyes.

Once I started letting go of people who didn't serve their purpose in my life any longer, I started to become whole. I started to see my worth after being blinded for too long. I began to breathe. I saw why loving people who give me no purpose only make self-love further away.

It took years of rockiness to let go of some who were always on the edge with my heart. I loved them very much, just not enough to let them go. I didn't think it was possible to walk away from people I promised to love forever.

*A message to anyone **learning** to love themselves,*

Self-love takes time and dedication. It takes failing and being damaged, to rebuild yourself again. It takes losing people you loved for decades and preventing new ones to leave a mark. It takes losing your worth to understand what you deserve. Sometimes you get everything taken from you to see the light. Sometimes you find the light before you lose yourself completely. It's a battlefield, you grow up learning to love everyone else so deeply, that you never were taught to give that same love to yourself. You fear being alone, the thought of being without anyone and focusing on yourself seems wrong. It's never selfish to love yourself and take time for yourself. You don't need anyone by your side to define you. You don't need anyone to love you to show you're worthy of being loved in return. Take that energy you're using on everyone else and give it to yourself. Take a step back, and focus on your being before you give an ounce of it to someone else. Watch how beautiful every connection grows after you set the foundation and know your worth. Yes, people will come in and out still, but you'll know not to let them overstay their welcome. You'll stand up for yourself when you're being walked over. You'll find that natural beauty. You'll feel beautiful just by feeding your soul exactly what it needs to fulfill your every need. It's not wrong to do what's best for you.

Note to self:

"I'm no longer that insecure girl who let every opinion change my reflection of myself.

I've found a balance in embracing my insecurities and knowing they're what makes me beautiful."

I've found love within. Your insecurities can't change my judgment on that love."

A note to you:

It's the hardest thing,
To love someone who hasn't found their purpose.
They'll reflect their insecurities on you,
In hopes, that your insecurities will shine brighter.

It's a battle,
Loving someone who's still battling to find that love
within themselves.

A message to my past self:

I've written this letter many different times. I've called myself a victim many times, with too many different heartbreaks, to become accountable for my many mistakes. I realized blaming you wasn't exactly how to heal, nor was blaming everyone. I found a way to heal once I learned to not place blame, it doesn't matter who's right and who's wrong. I hurt myself countless times letting myself get failed every time I gave myself to anyone, open-heartedly. In those other letters, I apologized to everyone I hurt, along with myself. I'm not writing this one to apologize. I want to acknowledge all perspectives, it's a part of the healing process. I don't need to bring up past pain. I don't need to remind you how strong you are, we've made it through, many times, and my strength doesn't need to be remembered. I don't need to keep reflecting on you as if you matter the most. I don't need to apologize to my past self, I was who I was meant to be at that time, and I can't change what already lived its purpose. I'm writing this letter to finally put you to rest, the wandering mind of the past, I'm letting you go. It's always been a thing for me, to reflect on, but this part of my life needs to be put behind me. I'm living in the present, it's a gift, a blessing. I don't live to prove to the past. I don't live to plan the future. I live for the moment, at the moment. I'm evolving, always.

Write a message to your past self:

_____

_____

_____

_____

_____

_____

_____

_____

_____

_____

_____

_____

_____

_____

A message to my present self:

I'm proud, to keep it short. Looking back to reflect is something I'm leaving in the past. Now, I'm reflecting on the moment. At this moment, I'm blessed and completely thankful to be living another day. Life has its stress, sometimes more overwhelming than usual. Sometimes the grip is hard to keep control of. Sometimes life slips through the cracks and I find myself in a mess. I haven't had many messes I had to clean up, life has been steady. We're currently going through a pandemic at this moment, but life has still made me thankful. I'm healthy, safe, and accepting of myself. I'm not so lost anymore. I know my worth and I haven't settled for anything since. I lost some of my greatest friends, so I thought they were, but life has been amazing since. I learned to not dwell in the absence of anyone who has dismissed themselves from my life. I learned to not hold anyone accountable for their outgrowing. I learned to hold close to everyone who reciprocates. I capture every moment as it comes. I soak up the love. I've found bravery in my vulnerability. I haven't once settled for someone's acceptance. I found wholeness alone, I found wholeness loving someone else- I know the difference. I've limited the impact my insecurities hold I try hard to overcome them. I have a positive mindset and I have my lows- balance keeps me sane. I keep people who inspire me around me and detach myself from anyone who tries to drown me. I'm steady where I need to be, but I'm only growing from here. I love the view.

Write a message to your present self:

_____

_____

_____

_____

_____

_____

_____

_____

_____

_____

_____

_____

_____

1.   What does self-love mean to you?

When I think of self-love, I think about the journey it took to get here. It's an endless journey of discovering your soul. As you grow, you learn new dimensions to you. I never liked the word change due to the fact we grow and not everyone just "changes" due to the season or being influenced. It's true, we have people we admire that we hold close and watch grow, some we wish we could be like. Once you get to a certain place in your life, you'll realize they can only impact you as much as you believe. That's why it's important to keep people around who positively inspire you. The people in your life have a big impact on your direction in life, don't lose sight of your direction, and let love blind you. No one who truly loves you will blind you from what's best for you.

Self-love is forever. It's something we will learn in parts. We fail, crash, and become lost. It's not something you'll discover, and have it passed you, you will always need to love yourself more. To sum it up, I would say it's giving up the love you always wanted to give to yourself. It's all about setting boundaries.

2.   What do you love about yourself?

I have thought about this so many times and every single time I add something different to the list. I love something new about myself all the time. Some of the things I couldn't stand are now something I've embraced. You need to fully get a full perspective of yourself before you can speak the most loved parts of you. You need to accept every part of your being before you can peacefully love yourself.

Things I tried to change about myself:

- **Being "too" emotional**

Everyone I got close enough to, to express my love in form of action, denied me. They would state I was "too emotional" for their liking. At the moment I wasn't thinking of the outcome, I just wanted to be loved, I wasn't thinking of loving someone with a cold heart. I don't know why I stayed once I felt how cold, but once I froze it was hard to melt. I let multiple people influence my judgment of my intuition and heart. I let myself turn to the dark side just to fill the void. I let myself turn cold, just to fit their standards, I didn't want to make them uncomfortable with my heart.

- **Tried gaining weight**

Public image was something so huge when I was growing up. People shamed some for being overweight but overlooked when someone spoke about someone being underweight. I never fought an eating disorder, but I fought the voices and opinions daily. It was an awkward experience, some people

would be jealous of the amount of food I could eat
without gaining weight, and some would play on it
like it was a sickness.

Questions like,

-   Why don't you gain weight?
-   Are you sick?
-   Are you depressed?
-   Are you not eating enough?
-   What size are you?

Or the remarks:

-   "Let me bring you to my family's house,
    they'll feed you"
-   "Let me cook you something"
-   You're so skinny!
-   "WOW, you're skinnier in person"
-   You look like you don't eat

I swear skinny shaming wasn't much thought back
when I was young. People didn't acknowledge it, nor
did they see the disrespect every time they asked me
one of those questions or opened their mouths with
one of their remarks. I was always taught if I didn't
have anything nice to say, not say it at all. I just wish
a lot of others shared that same experience. I am
someone who lets the emotions of the world get the
best of me. I take the stress of the world on my

shoulders. I act like it doesn't affect me, but it does, too much. It was shameful to know someone had never seen a skinny person before, by how they looked and spoke to me. Their opinions may have affected the way I envisioned myself at that very moment. I prayed I would gain some weight to look at the standards everyone had set for me. Instead, I found beauty in my skin. This is been the battle of my life, being 100 pounds until I was about 23. I'm now 26, no longer that skinny "underweight" girl. I'm happy with my body. I love it. I'm working more towards keeping it healthy, but the motivation of my everyday life interferes with that. I started to love my body once I let go of anyone who couldn't find the beauty in it. I fought too long to be at peace with my public image. I don't need someone telling me what to do, or not to do with it. I like to love it. I like to embrace every part of it.

- **Breakouts**

Acne was big time for me, my teenage years sucked mainly because of it. It's odd how many people turn you away because of it or don't even look your way. I never felt beautiful with it, and the more I got turned down because of it, only made it harder was to accept it. My teenage years were the hardest because it was the worse. Hormones are going crazy, growing into a woman. The hardest part wasn't *trying to make someone love me with it, it was looking into the mirror and trying to love myself through it. I couldn't see passed it. I turned down a lot of plans and refused to meet people I met online. I was scared to be looked at differently because of it. It's sad, the first question I'd ask myself was, "will they love or dismiss me for it" It was a constant battle. The little things people picked on you for as a kid are stuff that sticks with you forever. When we're young we create these insecurities based on opinions or insults of others. Everyone has a pair of eyes, but everyone has a different perception. I was trying so hard to be beautiful to others, I couldn't even look at myself in the mirror. I struggled to be natural, once I learned how to do makeup I couldn't unsee it. I covered myself up when I had the chance, sometimes I didn't leave without it. I realized how badly I treated my skin with the chemicals. There was no method to my madness. I drove myself far away from who I truly am, trying to be beautiful to people who will never see the true beauty within me. I opened my eyes and embraced my natural self once I treated my skin the way it deserved. It's always been a part of me. Before you complain about your one pimple, realize it's not the end of the world.*

Those are some of the biggest milestones I've made for myself. Some of the things I hated most about myself, I found love in. Public image was my main issue. One thing I never lost sight of, was my heart. I never had to second guess my intuition. Everyone I loved, I loved wholeheartedly. My heart always showed up when all of me couldn't.

I love how loyal I am
I love the strength of my heart
I love being compassionate
I love my strength
I love my determination
I love that I taught myself everything I tried to prove
I love having a wild, big heart
I love my flaws
I love being a free spirit
I love my institution
I love my passion, my drive
I love my talents

There are many things I love, but I was the hardest to accomplish. I have made it to a place I can say I love myself. Every day is a new day, something new may arise, but I'm here to defeat anything that comes in between that love.

3. What am I holding onto that isn't serving me anymore?

It's a question you need to ask yourself to start the healing process. The longer you hold onto anything that doesn't align with your growth, the harder it will be to grow. It may sound selfish to let go of time you gave so much energy to or someone you invested so much love in. It's the thing that will either make or break us, it's up to us how we let it affect us.

I walked away from people who I promised to love forever, at the time I didn't realize forever didn't exist within us. I may have forced more time when the universe showed me the signs to go. I may have over-loved who didn't even reciprocate half. I may have let my heart take over in situations I should have led with my intuition. I may have sacrificed my worth to fix a broken soul. I may have failed many times at setting boundaries. When it came to my love, I loved never in half, so, that right there shows my level of loyalty. I may hurt some along the way, it was never my intention, I just outgrew them. Love wasn't always the answer, love isn't always enough.

- **I resigned from jobs that no longer gave me the option to grow within.**

- **I got fired from jobs that didn't care enough for my whole being, sickness, or mental health.**

I stopped reaching out to people who didn't care to return the act of love.

- **I stopped trying for acceptance.**

- **I walked away from friendships that became acquaintances, more like strangers.**

- **I no longer communicate with family who disrespects my intelligence, or my being overall. Blood doesn't make family, connections do, and love does.**

- **I left behind old flames before they burnt me.**

You evolve every day, you may not see it up close, but you do. Simple things like getting rid of old clothes that don't fit you and buying new ones. Buying the everyday essentials. Indulging in new foods, sweets, or hobbies. Letting go and bringing in the new is always recommended. Stepping outside your comfort zone to try something new may be scary, but you'll embrace it with the worth it deserves. If you think of loving yourself the same way, you'll be a step closer to accepting yourself as a whole.

4. What Fulfills you?

Before you answer this, think about it for a minute. If the first thing that comes to your head is someone else, stop right there. When you put that kind of pressure on someone saying they're what fulfills you, it's meaningless if you don't name yourself.

What fulfills you shouldn't be defined by anyone or anything that adds to you. Yes, they're special. Yes, they add meaning to your life, but they don't fulfill you if you think of them before yourself. It's easy to get caught up in someone else when your heart takes over there's no telling. It's important to not get lost in your heart as you drown in the love you have for someone else. It's how many lose their purpose when they try and find fulfillment in others.

"How do you find what fulfills you"

Finding what fulfills you may take some time, especially if you're off-focus. It's a learning process. I believe that your purpose and what fulfills you tie into each other. I don't believe we were born with a purpose. I feel it's more the route we choose in life, our character, and our hidden talents that create our purpose. I wasn't born and knew I wanted to be a writer. I grew up wanting to be many different things, especially things that were input into my everyday life.

It wasn't until I was a teenager that I became obsessed with the art of music, and my gift of writing came to play. I still want to one day become a songwriter, I have many influences: Ne-Yo, Miguel,

DVSN, and The Weeknd. They all write their truth so beautifully; they are unapologetically them. The thing about inspiration is you don't wish to be them, you simply admire their work of art and wish to be at the level of acceptance they're at.

It's all about how you feel about yourself because it shows within their music how much they love their art. I feel their music like I wrote it myself. I believe that's an important thing to remember, don't become your inspiration, but admire them, let them inspire you, not influence you into wanting to be someone you're not. Your inspirations should open your eyes to the truth in who you are and the hidden talents within your soul.

Your purpose will only grow. Your fulfillment will only get deeper. Take a moment to yourself and think about everything you accomplished, everything that makes you a genuine soul. What you do for others, what you do for yourself. Think about your goals. Think about a moment in time you made yourself proud. These fulfilling moments will surprise you they will bring you a different perspective when it comes to your purpose. Notice yourself, own the beautiful soul and heart you were so rightfully blessed with. Everyone who walks into your life and loves you only adds to that purpose.

So now, tell me, what fulfills you?

_____

_____

_____

_____

_____

_____

_____

_____

_____

_____

_____

Your self-worth is the love that matters.

People who don't value you,

Won't love you either.

Self-love is hard to discover

You may search for years
to uncover that love.
If only it was as easy
as giving your heart
to the ones who didn't deserve it.

A love that's meant for you,
won't be presented to you
until you learn to love yourself.

You'll accept the love that's wrong for you
because you won't know what's right for you.

Practice self-love by taking care of yourself,
before taking care of anyone
who drives you to believe
their need is more important
than your sanity.

Your self-love journey Is the most important story
you live to tell. It's not a fairytale world,
You'll find yourself with your emotions all over the
place, you're human. You found the beauty in
yourself and conquered loving yourself through
every flaw.

Loving yourself not only brings confidence, but It also brings the strength to love another with the same love you give yourself Without taking away from the love you have for yourself.

Self-love is beautiful,
you should try it today.

Don't give up when times get rough,
and the days are looking dark.

Don't give up when you fall short of a goal you
should have accomplished months or years ago.

There's always more time.

Don't give up.

Be the one who loves unconditionally.
Be the one who always gives 100%.
Be the one who's true to yourself
and everyone you love.

Just be you,
don't change to fit into someone's life,
if it doesn't fit, it's not meant to.

Don't let the demons of your journey
bring you fear in accepting the truth
in whom you are,
where you want to be,
and where you're at now.

Trust the energy you give,
You will get that exact energy in return.
Love the ones who love you back,
Unconditionally.

Self-love is the hardest chapter
In your life to uncover.
There are many dimensions
to loving every part of you.

Accepting your flaws
and how they tie into your beauty.
Letting go of old habits
that created toxic behavior.

Bringing in the new,
the growth,
and lastly,
the love.

I can only take so much pain before I'm left with repairing my being. I can't keep being a shield from your destruction. I can't keep giving you all of me, just to have you take the last bit I'm holding onto.

Having a big heart isn't a burden, but sometimes it seems to be. If I push you away it's because I couldn't keep letting you take my worth with you.

If I push you away, you won't find me where you left me. I'm strong than I was every time I let you back in. I'm over trying to make you feel my love. What I gave wasn't enough.

I'm no longer a convenience.
So, don't get it twisted,
my heart is big,
It just doesn't beat for you any longer.

I'm giving my love to those
who won't abuse it,
starting with self.

My toxic trait was ghosting loved ones when I should have given that last word. Once words were spoken and lost, I thought setting myself free at any cost was all I had left. I'm holding love in my heart while wondering "what if" …

It's a bittersweet feeling, I did what I thought was best for me while being toxic to them. I didn't see another way out; I only saw a way through. Even though love still resides here, I'm at a place in life that wouldn't make sense to them, we grew apart.

It's true,

We're all toxic to someone, we all once hurt someone, and they saw us as the toxic one. I'm mature enough to take the blame. I know I might not be thinking of sparing their feelings, call me selfish but neither of us was a saint.

What I don't agree with, is being someone's every need and in return, being called "toxic" because I left but everything good, I brought suddenly vanished. I don't believe I'm perfect, trust me, but I knew my intentions.

I won't be deemed toxic to everyone. Some are quick to lie to me and forget they loved me. They forget the good just to paint the picture of being this saint while I'm damaged goods. Some may say you can't decide if you were toxic to someone, but I lived the story.

There are two sides to every story, yours and mine. The world has its opinions but theirs doesn't mean anything, compared to what I lived through, so no one can tell me what's best for me, or what I did was wrong. I know I could have handled some situations better. One thing I won't apologize for is not giving enough, knowing I gave more than I had to give. Just to get buried under your story of me, jokes on you, your side doesn't define me.

I know what I brought to us.
I see everything clearly,
back then I didn't.
Nothing can make me feel
what I did was wrong,
I chose what was calling me
what my heart needed.
I won't apologize for something
I'm not sorry,
just to spare your feelings.
If that makes me toxic,
look in the mirror.

We need to teach less self-destruction
and more self-love.
We need to stop giving ourselves
so easily to people with hearts
that don't match ours,
or aren't meant to fit.

We need to stop chasing.
We need to stop trying
to fill a void
that can only be discovered within.

There's always someone more beautiful
In your eyes,
because your insecurities speak louder.

Don't let your insecurities take you down
breakthrough,
I promise they won't break you.

Take a moment,
to appreciate your being.

Take a moment,
to soak in the feeling
of every emotion running through you.

Don't hide from the parts of you
that aren't accepted.

Don't hide from who you're destined to be,
trying to fit into society's expectations.

Don't let anyone distract you from yourself.
Be you,
Unapologetically, you.
Keep yourself afloat from misery.
Ones from the past may be bitter,
they once loved you,
but hate is a form of love.
Their reflection of you
is the pain they're hoarding.
Their demons aren't your problem.
Their version of you doesn't define you.
Your purpose makes them uncomfortable,
It's not your fault.

I remember trying to heal everyone who was broken until I realized I almost broke down trying to mend them back together. I try to fix something I didn't break. I chose to heal myself and not lose myself.

I always thought I could save anyone from their pain, or my love could erase their misery. I couldn't heal anyone nor was my love the answer. It didn't matter how much I loved them, their pride, ego, and lack of compassion for themselves ruined that love.

It doesn't matter the label, when you love someone, you love them. That's what holds significant meaning, the way you love everyone always comes out the same.

To everyone, I was close to,
Our memories are cherished,
But we've outgrown our time in this lifetime.

So,

Don't wait around for anyone to change, their growth isn't your job, nor is their healing. Don't feel bad for walking away when you need to better yourself. Don't let anyone drain you.

Live intensely,
So you don't have time to think about
analyzing every situation and decision.

Be fearless to weaknesses
and everything that's blocking you from loving
yourself.

You may need to let go of people who don't serve
the way your soul needs. The journey isn't easy,
you don't need to have it all figured out. That's
the beauty in life, not knowing what could
happen. Praying you'll figure it out.

Some people take forever to find self-love,
Some never understand.

I hope this message can somehow help you
understand that your impossible is possible.
Everything you want is well deserved if you
work for it, love it deeply, and love yourself fiercely.

I cried when I turned 25,
I was halfway to 50.
Terrified of growing old.
I just wish it didn't take so long to see.
How beautiful it was to
Love me,
To let go of some
and welcome new souls in.

I cried not knowing what 25 might bring,
but it brought me everything I needed.

Don't ever be afraid of change

Come back to this page when you need this reminder...

"Wake up today
And do your best to love yourself
Without hitting roadblocks
that leads you nowhere.
Stop loving people who only make it hard.

Love yourself today,
Tomorrow
And forever.

Promise me you'll try,
I promise you,
You'll fall in love with you"

Fill this page with daily affirmations for you

Continued... fill this page too:

What does self-love mean to you?

_____

_____

_____

_____

_____

_____

_____

_____

_____

_____

_____

_____

_____

What are you holding onto that isn't serving you anymore?

_____

_____

_____

_____

_____

_____

_____

_____

_____

_____

_____

What fulfills you?

_____

_____

_____

_____

_____

_____

_____

_____

_____

_____

_____

_____

What do you value about yourself?

_____

_____

_____

_____

_____

_____

_____

_____

_____

_____

_____

_____

What are you doing to invest in yourself,
how do you balance it with your relationships?

_____

_____

_____

_____

_____

_____

_____

_____

_____

_____

_____

Use this page for your fears:

Use this page for your doubts:

Use this page for your aspirations:

I hope this collection brought you peace.
Thank you for always giving my work a chance.
I hope you enjoyed the open space for you to
reflect and start or progress your healing
journey with my guidance.

All my platforms:

Instagram: Moonsoulchild
Twitter: Bymoonsoulchild
Facebook Moonsoulchild
Tiktok: Bymooonsoulchild
Apple Music: Moonsoulchild
Spotify: Moonsoulchild

Moonsoulchild.com

Made in the USA
Monee, IL
21 November 2023

47075770R00050